KinderSounds:

by Lillian Lieberman

illustrated by Marilynn Barr

Publisher: Roberta Suid
Copy Editor: Carol Whiteley
Design and Production: Little Acorn Associates, Inc.
Cover Design: David Hale

Call our toll-free number: 1-800-255-6049
E-mail us at: MMBooks@aol.com
Visit our Web site:
http://www.mondaymorningbooks.com

ISBN 1-57612-127-5

Printed in the United States of America
9 8 7 6 5 4 3 2 1

Contents

Introduction

KinderSounds: Games is a book of games and activities for preschool and kindergarten children that fosters and reinforces early learning of the sounds of the alphabet and rhyme. The activities in this book give young children opportunities to practice and strengthen their skills in initial phonemic awareness within an entertaining format. The engaging games and activities aid the teacher in guiding the children to become willing partners in learning.

KinderSounds: Games starts with several activities that give the young child experience in perceiving and discriminating rhyme elements. Working with a **jigsaw puzzle** format, the child names the pictures shown and listens for the rhyme elements in order to match the pieces. Reinforcement of rhyming elements then continues with **card games** such as "Rhyme-o Rummy" and "Rhyme Concentration" and **lace-ups** such as "Rhyme Lace-ups." In **board games** such as "Nuts and Rhymes," children spin a spinner and move a marker while supplying a rhyme.

A variety of additional hands-on experiences also provide children with opportunities to practice and reinforce the beginning consonant sounds. In simple **matching** games, such as "Muffins for the Moose," the child names the pictures and identifies the beginning consonant sound. **Slip-in** activities such as "Sand Crabs in the Sand" provide another enjoyable format in which the child slips in the matching pictures for an initial consonant sound.

File folder game set-ups also provide challenge, excitement, and active participation. In "Penguin Party," children move markers and follow directions. In "Spin and Fish," players spin a spinner and gather as many fish as they can. In "Dinosaur Den," children throw a die to get to the den. Finally, **sliders** give children a chance to practice the five short vowel sounds repeatedly. The child moves a slider and names the pictures that begin with a particular short vowel sound as they are exposed in the window.

As you begin to use the book, refer to the table of contents to see which activities target particular sounds. You may use and sequence the activities to fit the needs of the children. Before beginning an activity, help the children set out the game or materials and guide them through the "To Play" directions. Make sure that they have all the necessary game parts—markers, die, cards, etc. Train the children to store and put the game away after play. A basket or file box can be used for storage.

These games and activities are simple to construct using available materials and tools and the general and specific instructions. Some games will require the addition of markers or a die. Directions for playing and using the games are also given. The children will easily learn the games' repeated sequence and simple rules.

Awareness of the sounds of the alphabet and rhyme is an important first step towards success with phonics skills. The high-interest games and activities in *KinderSounds: Games* will make learning an enjoyable experience through active play and stimulation. The games and activities can be used in both the regular and the special resource classroom and are ideal for learning centers.

Muffins for the Moose

How to Make the Activities: General Directions

Materials:
You will need glue sticks, sharp scissors, a craft knife, oak tag, file folders, clasp envelopes, colored felt pens, and colored pencils or crayons. Some games require markers or die and brass fasteners for spinners.

To Make:
Duplicate the games and activities. Glue to oak tag or to file folders as instructed in the Specific Directions. Color and trim. Cut out the parts. Laminate if desired. Store the game or game parts in a clasp envelope. For file folder games, glue the envelope to the back of the file folder. Glue the playing directions to the front of the envelope or to the front of the file folder. For specific directions for each type of game or activity, follow the Specific Directions below.

Specific Directions

Jigsaw Puzzles:
Duplicate the puzzle. Glue to oak tag. Cut out the parts and enclose in a clasp envelope. Glue the playing directions to the front of the envelope.

Card Games:
Duplicate the cards. Glue to oak tag. Cut out the cards. Enclose in a clasp envelope. Cut out the playing directions and glue to the front of the envelope.

Matching Activities:
Duplicate the activity. Glue to oak tag or to file folders as specified. Cut out the parts and enclose in a clasp envelope. Glue the playing directions to the front of the envelope.

Lace-ups:

Duplicate the activity. Glue to oak tag. Trim and cut out the lace-up card. Punch holes where indicated. Insert yarn or a shoelace into the hole and knot in the back. Secure with tape. If using yarn, wrap a piece of transparent tape around the loose end to keep it from fraying. Enclose the lace-up in a clasp envelope. Glue the playing directions to the front of the envelope.

File Folder Board Games:

Duplicate the game set-up. Make additional copies where indicated. Trim the game. Assemble and glue to the inside of a file folder. Cut out the loose game parts and enclose in a clasp envelope. Glue the envelope to the back of the file folder. Glue the game illustration and the playing directions to the front of the file folder. Glue the game label on the file tab. These games require a spinner, markers, and/or a die.

For spinner games: Punch a hole in the spinner wheel and the spinner using the sharp end of a pair of scissors. If possible, trim around the hole with a pair of manicure scissors to make the spinner spin smoothly. Fasten the spinner to the wheel with a brass fastener.

For marker games: Provide the markers if not provided. Markers are available at teacher supply stores, or buttons, beans, or math counters may be substituted.

For die games: Provide the die. Dies are available at teacher supply stores or game stores.

Slip-ins:

Duplicate the activity. Glue to oak tag and trim. Use a craft knife to cut on the dotted lines for the slip-in. Glue the activity in a file folder. Leave the area around the slip-in free of glue. Cut out the loose game parts and enclose in a clasp envelope. Glue the envelope to the back of the file folder. Glue the playing directions to the front of the file folder. Cut out the game label and glue to the file tab.

Sliders:

Duplicate the set-up for each slider activity. Glue to oak tag and cut out. Use a craft knife to cut on the dotted lines for the slots. Slip the picture panel through the slots so that the pictures show in the window. Enclose the slider in a clasp envelope. Cut out the playing directions and glue to the front of the envelope.

Tic-Tac-Toe Games:

Duplicate the Tic-Tac-Toe playing card. Glue to oak tag. For WINGO, cut out the picture cards. Provide nine markers per player. Enclose the game in a clasp envelope. Cut out the playing directions and glue to the front of the envelope.

Jigsaw Rhyme Match:

Give the children these directions: Two players may play. Mix pieces and place face down in rows. Take turns turning over two pieces at a time. If the picture names rhyme, put the pieces together and keep them. Say the rhyme names. If the pictures do not match, put the pieces back. The player with the most matches wins.

KinderSounds: Games © 2001 Monday Morning Books, Inc.

Jigsaw Rhyme Match

Jigsaw Rhyme Match

To Play:

Two players may play. Mix pieces and place face down in rows. Take turns turning over two pieces at a time. If the picture names rhyme, put the pieces together and keep them. Say the rhyme names. If the pictures do not match, put the pieces back. The player with the most matches wins.

Jigsaw Rhyme Match

KinderSounds: Games © 2001 Monday Morning Books, Inc.

Rhyme Lace-ups

Two players may play. Each player takes a Rhyme Lace-up card and names the pictures. Players match the pictures whose names rhyme by placing the lace into the appropriate hole.

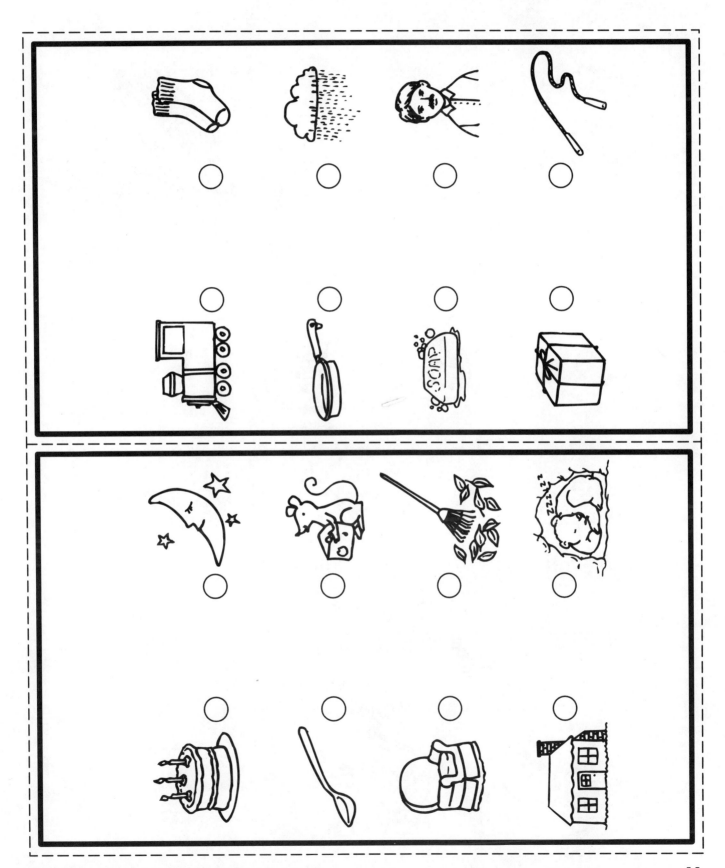

Rhyme Concentration

Two or three players may play. Place the Rhyme Concentration cards face down in rows. Each player turns over two cards in turn. If the picture names rhyme, the player keeps the two cards. If they do not rhyme, the player puts the cards back. The player with the most cards wins.

KinderSounds: Games © 2001 Monday Morning Books, Inc.

Rhyme Concentration

Rhyme-o Rummy

Rhyme-o Rummy

To Play:

Two players may play. Shuffle the Rhyme-o Rummy cards. Pass out five cards to each player. Place the rest of the cards in a pile face down. Each player looks at the pictures on his/her cards to find rhyme matches. If the picture names of two cards rhyme, the player says the rhymes, makes a book, and sets them aside. Each player in turn takes a card from the pile and checks for a rhyme match. Players must say the rhyme match names when they make a book. When there are no more cards in the pile, players may pick cards from each other. Pick from left to right. The player who gets rid of all his/her cards first is the winner.

To Make:

Duplicate the Rhyme-o Rummy cards. Glue to colored construction paper. Color and laminate if desired. Cut and trim. Place in a manila clasp envelope. Glue the playing instructions to the front of the envelope.

Rhyme-o Rummy

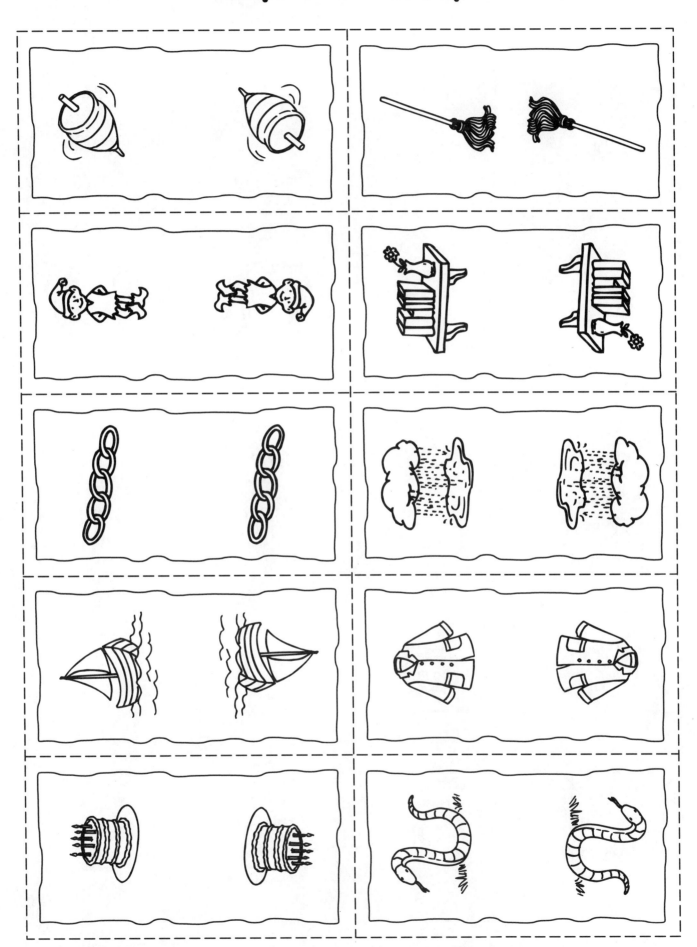

Rhyme-o Rummy

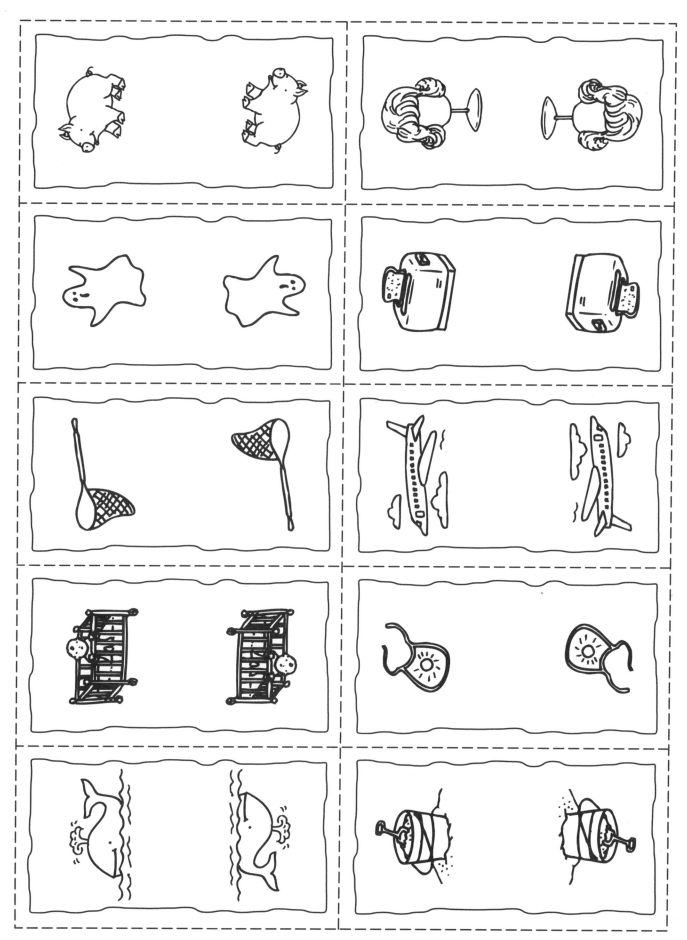

Nuts and Rhymes

(Identifying and Naming Rhymes)

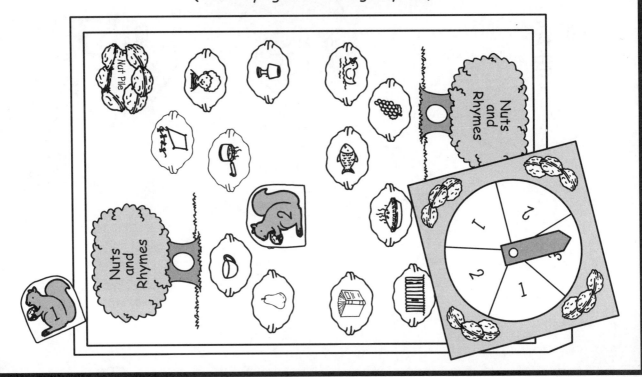

To Play:

Two players may play. Players choose a side of the file folder to play. Each takes a squirrel marker and places it on his/her nut pile. Each in turn spins the spinner. Players advance the number of nut spaces that the spinner points to. To place their marker on the nut, they must give a word that rhymes with the name of the picture on the nut, for example, cat/hat. If a player cannot give a rhyme, he/she misses a turn. The winner is the first player to reach his/her tree. The player must spin the exact number of spaces to get to the tree.

To Make:

Duplicate the game board set-up. Color, trim, and glue inside a file folder. Duplicate and color the spinner, wheel, and squirrel markers. Glue to oak tag and cut out. Punch holes in wheel and spinner. Fasten spinner to wheel with a brass fastener. Glue a clasp envelope to the back of the file folder. Store loose game parts in the envelope. Glue the game illustration and the playing instructions to the front of the file folder and the game label on the tab.

Nuts and Rhymes

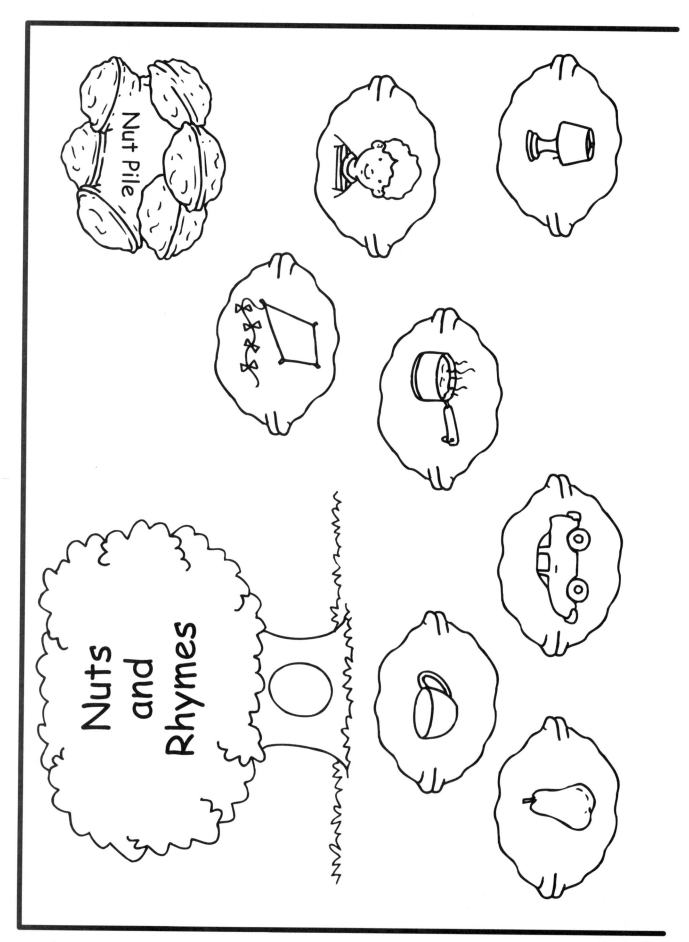

Nut Pile

Nuts and Rhymes

KinderSounds: Games © 2001 Monday Morning Books, Inc.

Nuts and Rhymes

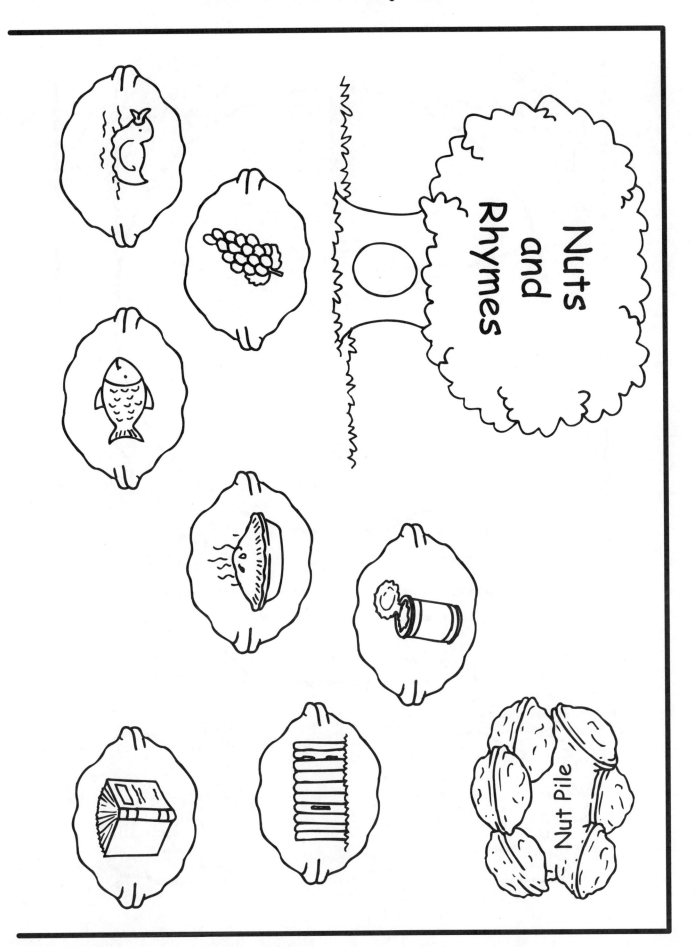

Nuts and Rhymes

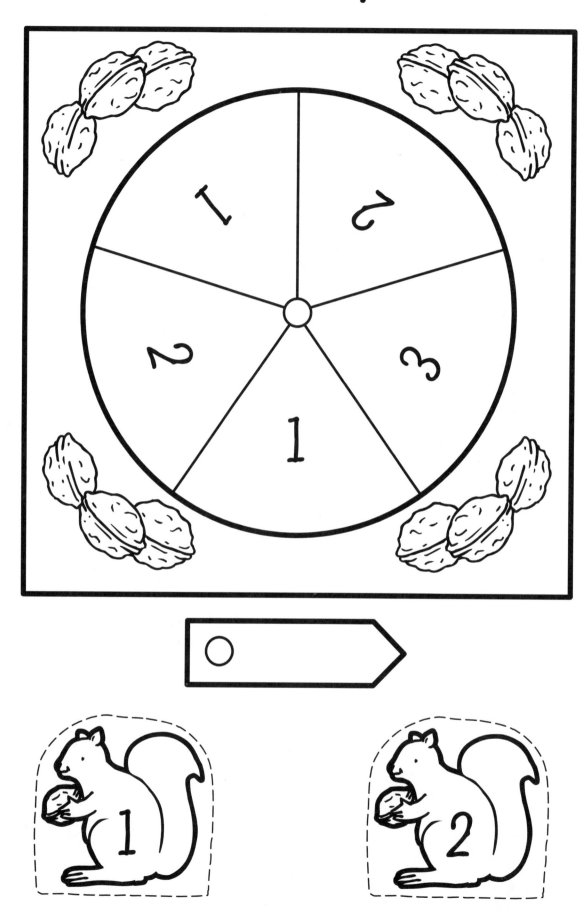

Big Balloons

(Initial Consonant b)

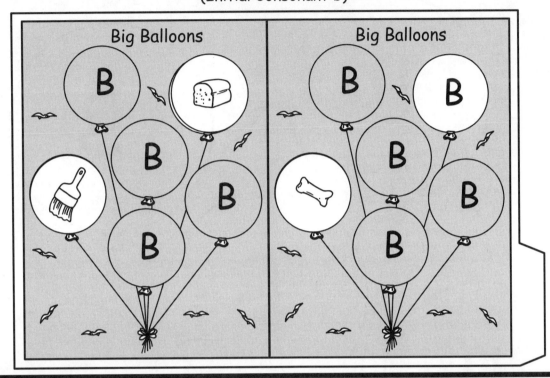

To Play:

Two players may play. Set up the game board in the playing area. Take out the picture circles and mix them. Place them in rows face down in the playing area. Each player chooses a set of balloons to play. Each player in turn takes a picture circle and names the picture. If the picture name begins with the b sound, the player puts the picture on one of his/her balloons. If the name does not begin with the b sound, the picture is placed back in the row. The winner is the first player who fills up all his/her balloons.

To Make:

Make two copies of the Big Balloons game set-up. Color and trim. Glue the set-ups inside a file folder, one on each side. Duplicate the picture circles and glue to oak tag. Color if desired. Cut out the circles and place in a clasp envelope. Glue the envelope to the back of the file folder. Duplicate the illustration, game directions, and game label. Cut out the illustration and game directions. Glue to the front of the file folder. Cut out the label and glue to the file tab.

Big Balloons

Duplicate two times.

Big Balloons

Big Balloons

Big Balloons

Cookie Car

(Initial Consonant Sound for Hard c)

To Play:

Two players may play. Take out the Cookie Car playing card, markers, and die. Give each player a marker. Each player puts a marker on Start. Each player in turn throws the die. Players go the number of spaces indicated on the die. The player names the picture on the space he/she lands on. Picture names all begin with the hard c sound, /k/. If a player does not say the correct word with the hard c sound, he/she must go back to Start. If a player lands on a numbered space, he/she must go that many spaces in the direction the arrow points. The first player to get to the Cookie Car is the winner. The player must throw the exact number to get to the Cookie Car.

To Make:

Duplicate the Cookie Car playing card. Glue to oak tag and trim. Provide two markers and a die. Enclose playing card, markers, and die in a clasp envelope. Duplicate the playing directions and glue to the front of the envelope.

Cookie Car

Dinosaur Den

(Initial Consonant d)

To Play:

Three players may play. Set up the game board in the playing area. Take out the die and three markers. Each player takes a marker and places it on Start. Each player in turn throws the die. Each player goes the number of spaces indicated on the die and places his/her die on the space. If there is a picture on the space, the player must name the picture for the d sound. If there is an arrow and a number on the space, the player must go that many spaces in the direction the arrow points. If the space is occupied by another marker, the player cannot go in that space and must remain in the space before it. The first player to get to the Dinosaur Den is the winner. The player must throw the exact number of spaces to get to the den.

To Make:

Duplicate the game set-up. Color and trim. Glue the set-up inside a file folder. Provide three markers and a die. Glue a clasp envelope to the back of the file folder. Enclose the three markers and the die in the envelope. Duplicate the illustration, game directions, and game label. Cut out the illustration and game directions. Glue to the front of the file folder. Cut out the label and glue to the file tab.

Dinosaur Den

Provide a die and three markers.

Start

Dinosaur Den

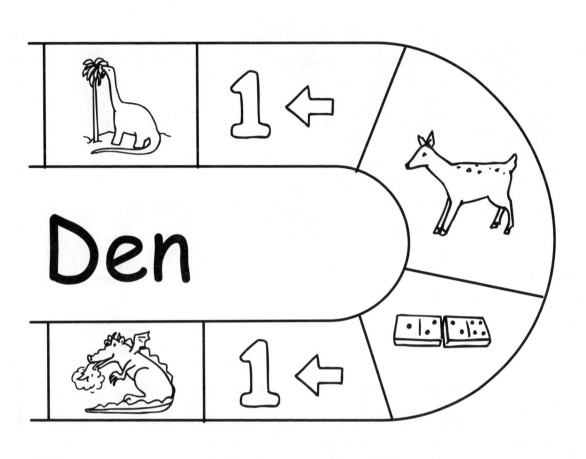

Den

Spin and Fish

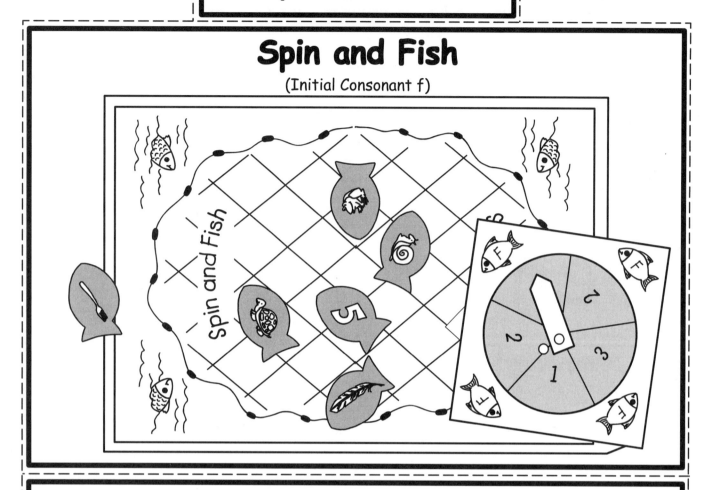

Spin and Fish
(Initial Consonant f)

To Play:

Three players may play. Set up the game board in the playing area. Take out the fish and the spinner. Mix the fish. Place them face down on the big fish net on the board. Each player in turn spins the spinner. Players take as many fish from the net as the spinner indicates. Players must name the picture on each fish. If the picture name begins with the f sound, the player keeps the fish. If the picture name does not begin with the f sound, the fish is discarded. The winner is the player with the most fish.

To Make:

Make two copies of the Spin and Fish game set-up. Color and trim. Glue the set-ups inside a file folder, one on each side. Duplicate the fish and the spinner set-up and glue to oak tag. Color if desired. Cut out the fish and the spinner set-up. Punch a hole in the spinner and the wheel. Attach the spinner to the wheel with a brass fastener. Place the loose game parts in a clasp envelope. Glue the envelope to the back of the file folder. Duplicate the illustration, game directions, and game label. Cut out the illustration and game directions. Glue to the front of the file folder. Cut out the label and glue to the file tab.

Spin and Fish

Duplicate two times.

Spin and Fish

Spin and Fish

Spin and Fish

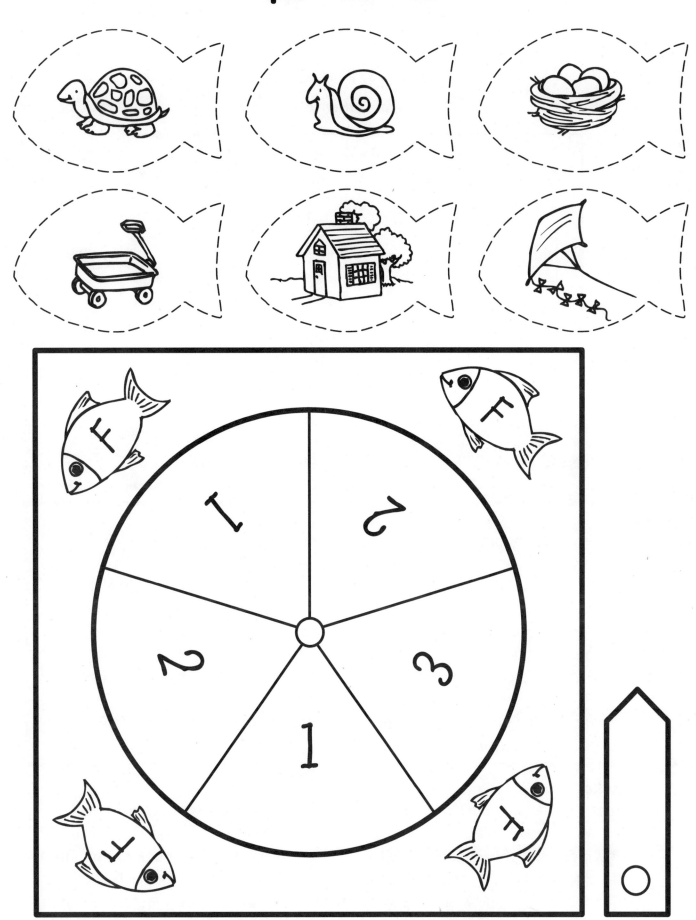

Bag of Gold

Bag of Gold

(Initial Consonant g)

To Play:

Three players may play. Set up the game board in the playing area. Take out the die, the three markers, and the gold coins. Place the gold coins on the bag of gold at the end of the game path. Each player takes a marker and places it on Start. Each player in turn throws the die. Each player goes the number of spaces indicated on the die and places his/her die on the space. If there is a picture on the space, the player must name the picture for the initial g sound. If there is a gold coin on the space with a number on it, the player takes that many gold coins from the bag of gold. The first player to reach the bag of gold is the winner. The player must throw the die the exact number of spaces. The winner gets all the coins remaining on the bag of gold.

To Make:

Duplicate the game board set-up. Color and trim. Glue the set-up inside a file folder. Make two copies of the gold coins. Glue them to oak tag and cut out. Provide a die and three markers. Glue a clasp envelope to the back of the file folder. Enclose the die, the markers, and the coins in the envelope. Duplicate the illustration, game directions, and game label. Cut out the illustration and the game directions. Glue to the front of the file folder. Cut out the label and glue to the file tab.

KinderSounds: Games © 2001 Monday Morning Books, Inc.

Bag of Gold

Provide a die and three markers.

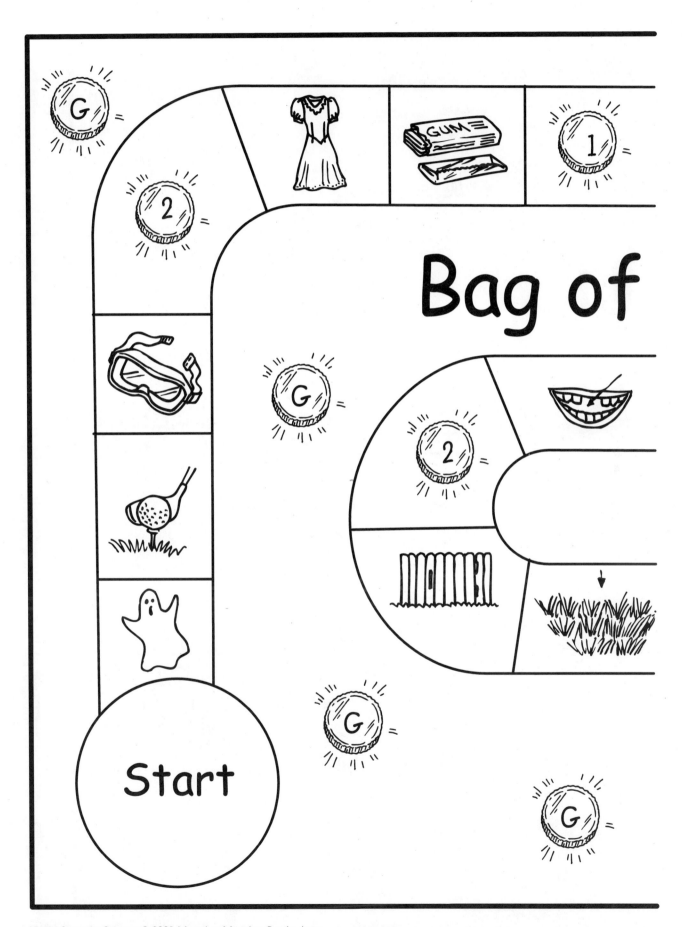

Bag of Gold

Gold

Bag of Gold

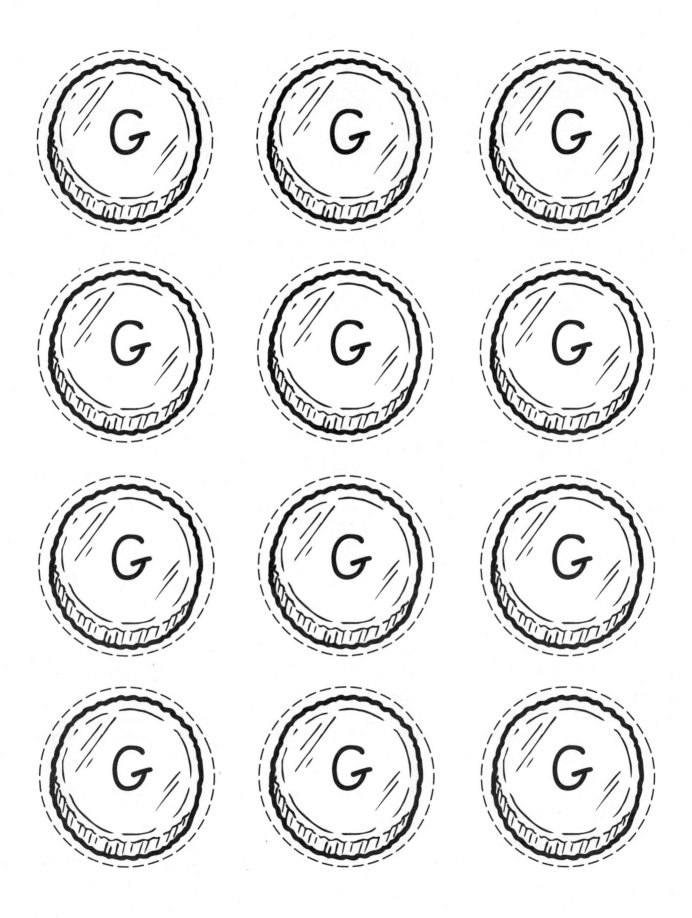

Have a Heart

Have a Heart

To Play:
Two players may play. Take out the hearts and mix them. Place the cards face down in rows in the playing area. Each player in turn takes a heart and names the picture on the heart. If the picture name begins with the h sound, the player keeps the heart. If the picture name does not begin with the h sound, the player discards the card. When all the hearts have been picked, each player counts his/her hearts. The player who ends up with the most hearts is the winner.

To Make:
Duplicate the hearts. Glue to oak tag or colored construction paper. Cut out. Enclose the hearts in a clasp envelope. Duplicate the game directions. Cut out and glue to the front of the envelope.

Have a Heart

Have a Heart

Jellybean Jar

Jellybean Jar
(Initial Consonant j)

To Play:

Two players may play. Put the game board in the playing area. Take out the jellybean picture shapes. Place the shapes face down in rows. Each player chooses a jellybean jar to play. Each player in turn takes a jellybean shape. If the jellybean has a picture whose name begins with the j sound, the player puts it on one of the jellybeans on his/her jar. If the picture name does not begin with the j sound, the player puts the jellybean back in the row. The first player to fill his/her jellybean jar is the winner.

To Make:

Make two copies of the Jellybean Jar game set-up. Color if desired. Trim and glue to the inside of a file folder, one jellybean jar on each side. Duplicate the jellybeans and glue to oak tag. Color if desired. Cut and place in a clasp envelope. Glue the envelope to the back of the file folder. Duplicate the illustration, the game directions, and the game label. Cut out the illustration and the directions. Glue to the front of the file folder. Cut out the label and glue to the file tab.

Jellybean Jar

Jellybean Jar

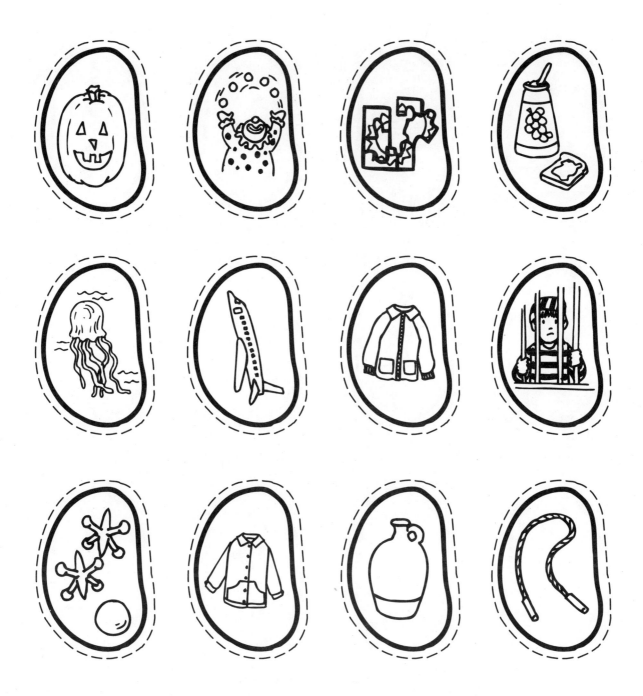

Jellybean Jar

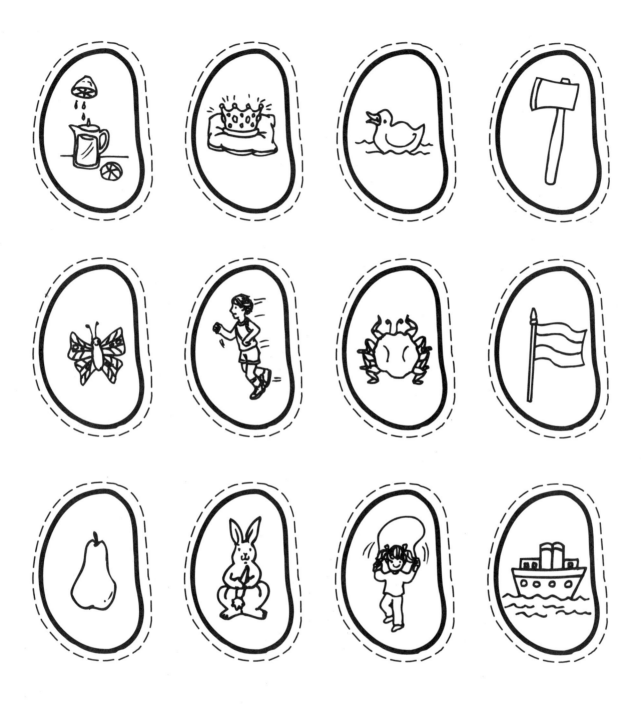

Kangaroo Kickball

Kangaroo Kickball

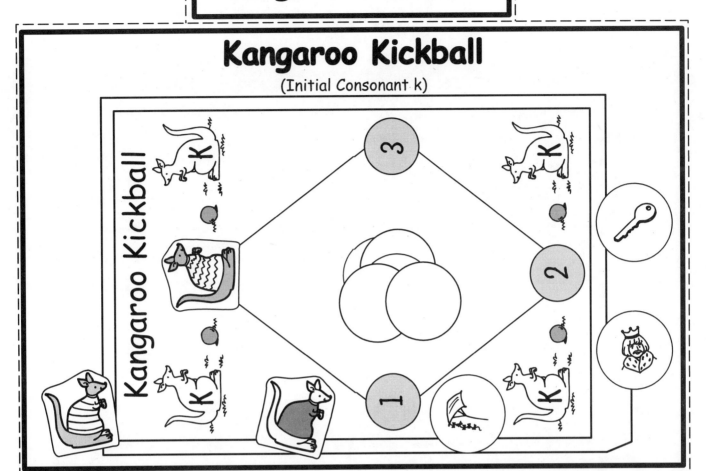

(Initial Consonant k)

To Play:

Three players may play. Set up the game board in the playing area. Take out the picture circles and kangaroo markers. Mix the picture circles. Place the picture circles face down in a pile on the Pitcher's Circle. Each player takes a marker and places it on Start. Each player in turn takes a picture circle and names the picture on it. If the name begins with the k sound, the player may move one base. If the name does not begin with the sound of k, the player may not move to a base. Cards played are put in a discard pile. The first player to get back to Start is the winner. The game may be played several times. Mix the circles at the start of each new game.

To Make:

Duplicate the game set-up. Color and trim. Glue the set-up inside a file folder. Duplicate the picture circles and the kangaroo markers. Glue to oak tag and cut out. Enclose the circles and markers in a clasp envelope. Glue the envelope to the back of the file folder. Duplicate the illustration, game directions, and game label. Cut out the illustration and game directions. Glue to the front of the file folder. Cut out the label and glue to the file tab.

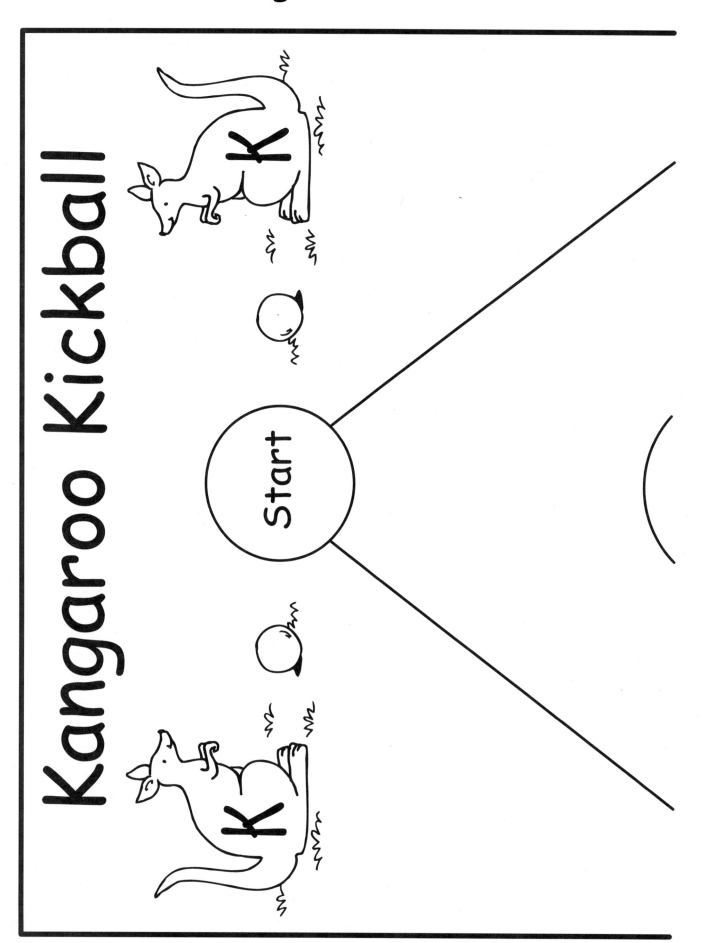

Kangaroo Kickball

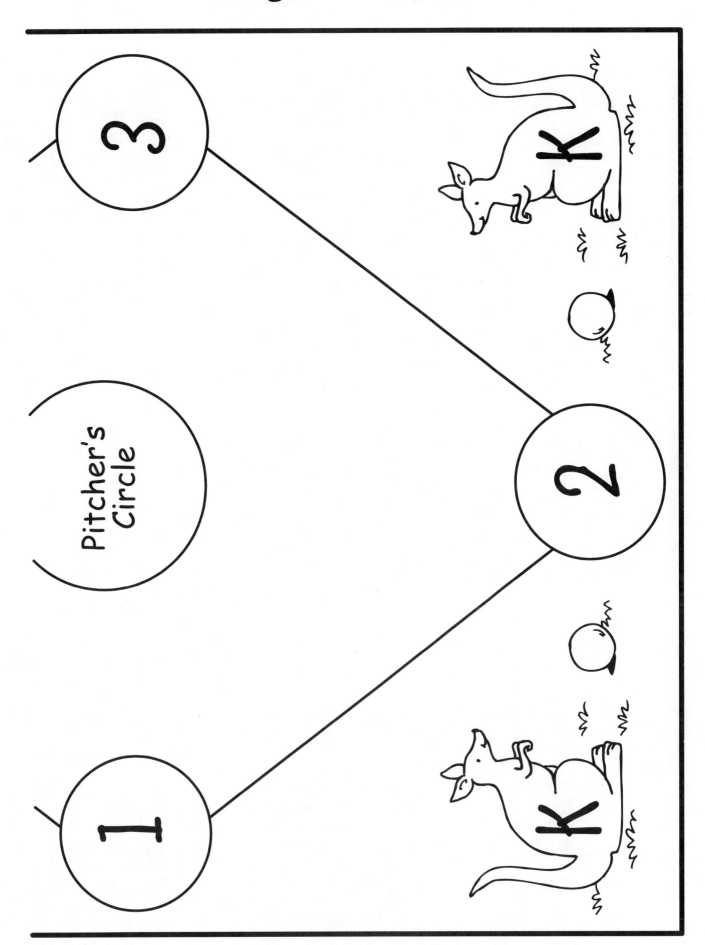

Kangaroo Kickball

Kangaroo Kickball

Lollipop Land

(Initial Consonant l)

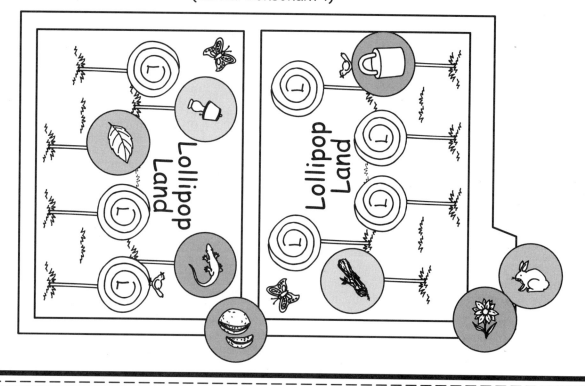

To Play:

Two players may play. Set up the game set-up in the playing area. Take out the picture circles and mix them. Place them in rows face down in the playing area. Each player chooses a Lollipop Land card to play. Each player in turn takes a picture circle and names the picture on it. If the picture name begins with the l sound, the player puts the picture on one of his/her lollipops. If the name does not begin with the l sound, the picture is placed back in the row. The winner is the first player who fills all his/her lollipops.

To Make:

Make two copies of the Lollipop Land game set-up. Color and trim. Glue the set-ups inside a file folder, one on each side. Duplicate the picture circles and glue to oak tag. Cut out the circles and place in a clasp envelope. Glue the envelope to the back of the file folder. Duplicate the illustration, game directions, and game label. Cut out the illustration and the game directions. Glue to the front of the file folder. Cut out the label and glue to the file tab.

Lollipop Land

Duplicate two times.

Lollipop Land

Muffins for the Moose

(Initial Consonant m)

To Play:

Two players may play. Set up the playing board in the playing area. Take out the muffins and mix them. Place them in rows face down in the playing area. Each player chooses a side of the board to play. Each player in turn takes a muffin and names the picture on it. If the name begins with the m sound, the player places it on a blank muffin on his/her playing board. If the name does not begin with the m sound, the muffin is placed back in the row. The first player to fill all his/her muffins is the winner.

To Make:

Make two copies of the Muffins for the Moose playing set-up. Color and trim. Glue the copies inside a file folder, one on each side. Duplicate the muffins and glue to oak tag. Color if desired. Cut out the muffins and place in a clasp envelope. Glue the envelope to the back of the file folder. Duplicate the illustration, game directions, and game label. Cut out the illustration and game directions. Glue to the front of the file folder. Cut out the label and glue to the file tab.

Duplicate two times.

Muffins for the Moose

Muffins for the Moose

Muffins for the Moose

Nests and Eggs

(Initial Consonant n)

To Play:

Two players may play. Set up the game board in the playing area. Take out the eggs and mix them. Place them in rows face down in the playing area. Each player chooses a set of nests to play. Each player in turn takes an egg and names the picture on it. If the picture begins with the n sound, the player slips the egg into one of his/her nests. If the name does not begin with the n sound, the egg is placed back in the row. The first player to fill all his/her nests with eggs is the winner.

To Make:

Make two copies of the Nests and Eggs game set-up. Color and trim. Glue the set-ups to oak tag. Cut on dotted line for slip-ins. Glue the set-ups inside a file folder, one on each side. Leave the area around the slots on the nests free of glue. Duplicate the eggs and glue to oak tag. Cut out and place in a clasp envelope. Glue the envelope to the back of the file folder. Duplicate the illustration, game directions, and game label. Cut out the illustration and game directions. Glue to the front of the file folder. Cut out the label and glue to the file tab.

Nests and Eggs
Duplicate two times. Glue to oak tag. Cut slots on the dotted lines.
Glue inside a file folder. Leave the area around the slots free of glue.

Nests and Eggs

KinderSounds: Games © 2001 Monday Morning Books, Inc.

Nests and Eggs

Penguin Party
(Initial Consonant p)

To Play:

Three players may play. Put the game board in the playing area. Mix the picture cards and put face down in a pile. Each player takes a penguin marker and places it on Start. Each player in turn takes a card from the pile. If the card has a picture whose name begins with the p sound, the player moves one space on the game board. The player must say the word to check. If the picture name does not begin with the p sound, the player may not move. If a player picks up a card with an arrow, he/she moves one space in the direction the arrow points. If the card has a Danger sign, the player loses a turn. All cards go into a discard pile. The discard pile may be put into play if there are no more cards to play. The first player to get to Stop is the winner.

To Make:

Duplicate the game board set-up. Trim and glue to a file folder. Duplicate the picture cards, direction cards, and penguin markers. Glue to oak tag. Color if desired. Cut and place the cards and the markers in a clasp envelope and glue the envelope to the back of the file folder. Duplicate the illustration, game directions, and game label. Cut out the illustration and the directions. Glue to the front of the file folder. Cut out the label and glue to the file tab.

Penguin
Party

Penguin Party

Penguin Party

Penguin Party

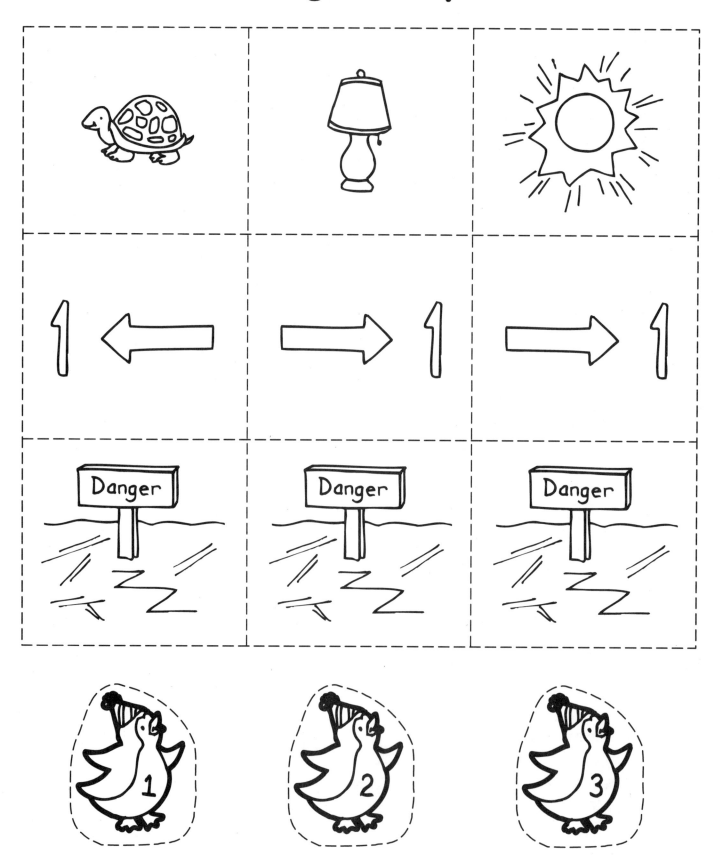

 KinderSounds: Games © 2001 Monday Morning Books, Inc.

The Queen's Quilt

(Initial Consonant q)

To Play:
Two players may play. Set up the game in the playing area. Take out the picture cards and mix them. Place them in rows face down in the playing area. Each player chooses a Queen's Quilt to play. Each player in turn takes a picture card and names the picture. If the picture name begins with the q sound, the player puts the card on one of the patches on his/her quilt. If the name does not begin with the q sound, the picture card is placed back in the row. The winner is the player with the most q picture cards.

To Make:
Make two copies of the Queen's Quilt set-up. Color and trim. Glue the set-ups inside a file folder, one on each side. Duplicate the picture cards and glue to oak tag. Cut out the cards and place in a clasp envelope. Glue the envelope to the back of the file folder. Duplicate the illustration, game directions, and game label. Cut out the illustration and game directions. Glue to the front of the file folder. Cut out the label and glue to the file tab.

Duplicate two times.

The Queen's Quilt

The Queen's Quilt

Ride the Rainbow

(Initial Consonant r)

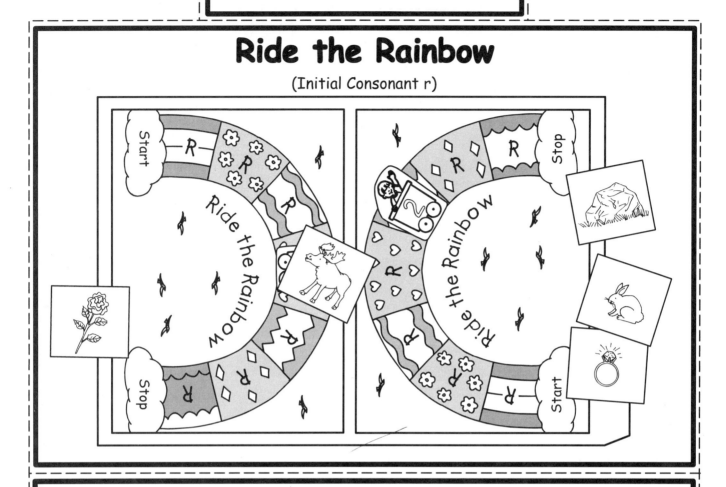

To Play:

Two players may play. Set up the game board in the playing area. Take out the picture cards and the two markers. Mix the picture cards and place face down in rows. Each player chooses a rainbow to play. Players put their marker on Start on their rainbow. Each player in turn picks a picture card and names the picture. If the picture name begins with the r sound, the player moves his/her marker one space on the rainbow. If the picture name does not begin with the r sound, the card is discarded and the player loses a turn. The first player to reach Stop is the winner.

To Make:

Make two copies of the game set-up. Color and trim. Glue to the inside of a file folder, one on each side. Duplicate the picture cards and the markers. Glue to oak tag and cut out. Enclose in a clasp envelope. Glue the envelope to the back of the file folder. Duplicate the illustration, game directions, and game label. Cut out the illustration and the game directions. Glue to the front of the file folder. Cut out the label and glue to the file tab.

Ride the Rainbow

Duplicate two times.

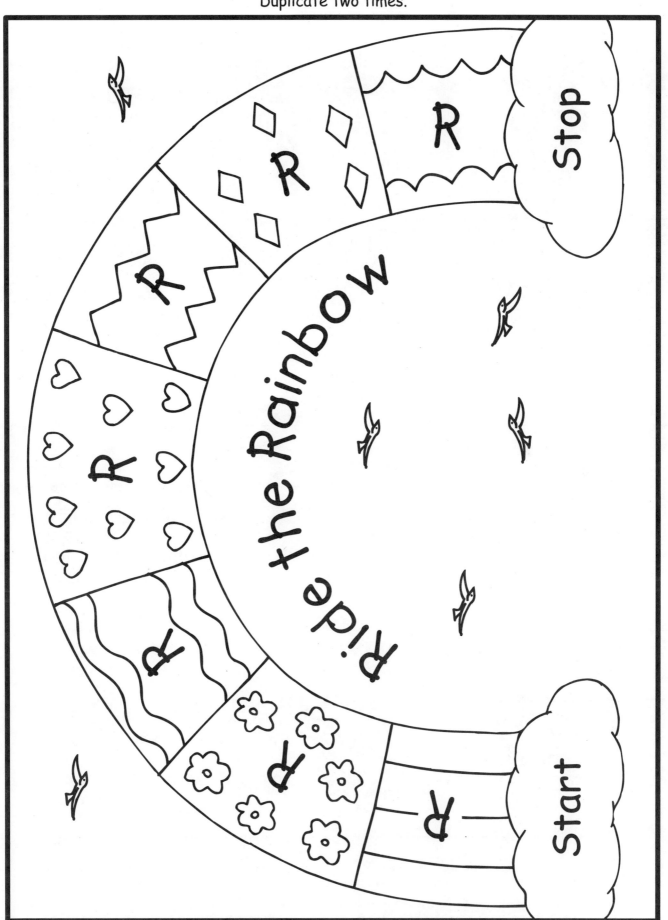

Ride the Rainbow

Ride the Rainbow

Sand Crabs in the Sand

(Initial Consonant s)

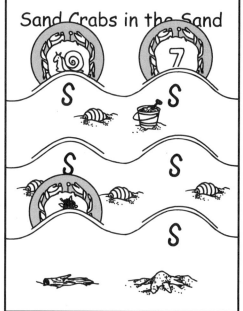

To Play:

Two players may play. Set up the game board in the playing area. Take out the sand crabs and mix them. Place them in rows face down in the playing area. Each player chooses a side of the game board to play. Each player in turn takes a crab and names the picture on it. If the name begins with the s sound, the player slips the crab into a sand mound. If the name does not begin with the s sound, the crab is placed back in the row. The winner is the first player to fill all his/her sand mounds.

To Make:

Make two copies of the Sand Crabs in the Sand game set-up. Glue to oak tag. Color and trim. Cut slots on the dotted lines. Glue the set-ups inside a file folder, one on each side. Leave the area around the slots on the sand mounds free of glue. Duplicate the sand crabs and glue to oak tag. Cut out the crabs and place in a clasp envelope. Glue the envelope to the back of the file folder. Duplicate the illustration, the game directions, and the game label. Cut out the illustration and the game directions. Glue to the front of the file folder. Cut out the label and glue to the file tab.

Sand Crabs in the Sand

Make two copies. Glue to oak tag. Cut slots on the dotted lines.

Sand Crabs in the Sand

Sand Crabs in the Sand

Sand Crabs in the Sand

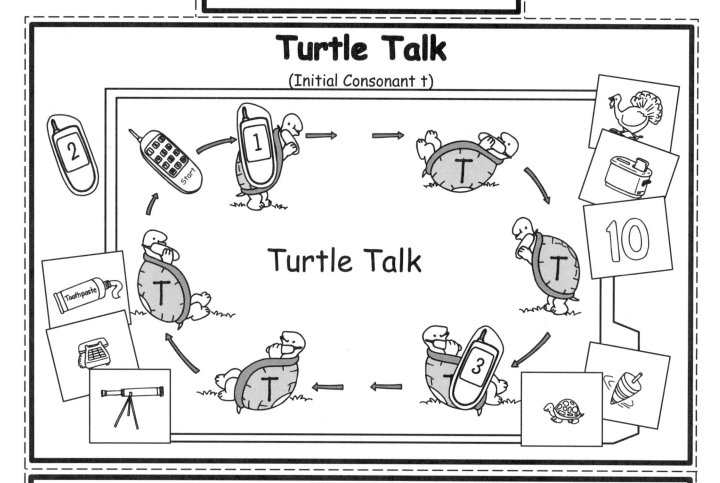

Turtle Talk

(Initial Consonant t)

Turtle Talk

To Play:

Three players may play. Put the game board in the playing area. Mix the picture cards and put them face down in a pile. To start, each player takes a telephone marker and places it on the big telephone on the game board. Players in turn take a picture card from the pile. If the card has a picture whose name begins with the t sound, the player moves his/her marker to the nearest turtle following the arrow. The player must say the word to check. If the picture name does not begin with the t sound, the player may not move the marker. All cards go into a discard pile. The discard pile may be put into play if there are no more cards to play. The first player to get back to the telephone is the winner.

To Make:

Duplicate the game board set-up. Trim and glue onto a file folder. Duplicate the picture cards and the telephone markers. Glue to oak tag. Color if desired. Place the cards and the markers in a clasp envelope and glue the envelope to the back of the file folder. Duplicate the illustration, game directions, and game label. Cut out the illustration and directions. Glue to the front of the file folder. Cut out the label and glue to the file tab.

Turtle Talk

Turtle

Turtle Talk

Talk

Turtle Talk

Turtle Talk

Violet's Van

Violet's Van
(Initial Consonant v)

To Play:

Two players may play. Set up the game in the playing area. Take out the picture cards and mix them. Place them in rows face down in the playing area. Each player chooses a van to play. Each player in turn takes a picture card and names the picture on it. If the picture name begins with the v sound, the player places it on one of the spaces on his/her van. If the picture does not begin with the v sound, the card is discarded. The winner is the first player who fills all his/her spaces on the van.

To Make:

Make two copies of the Violet's Van game set-up. Color and trim. Glue the set-ups inside a file folder, one on each side. Duplicate the picture cards and glue to oak tag. Cut out the squares and place in a clasp envelope. Glue the envelope to the back of the file folder. Duplicate the illustration, game directions, and game label. Cut out the illustration and the game directions. Glue to the front of the file folder. Cut out the label and glue to the file tab.

Violet's Van

Duplicate two times.

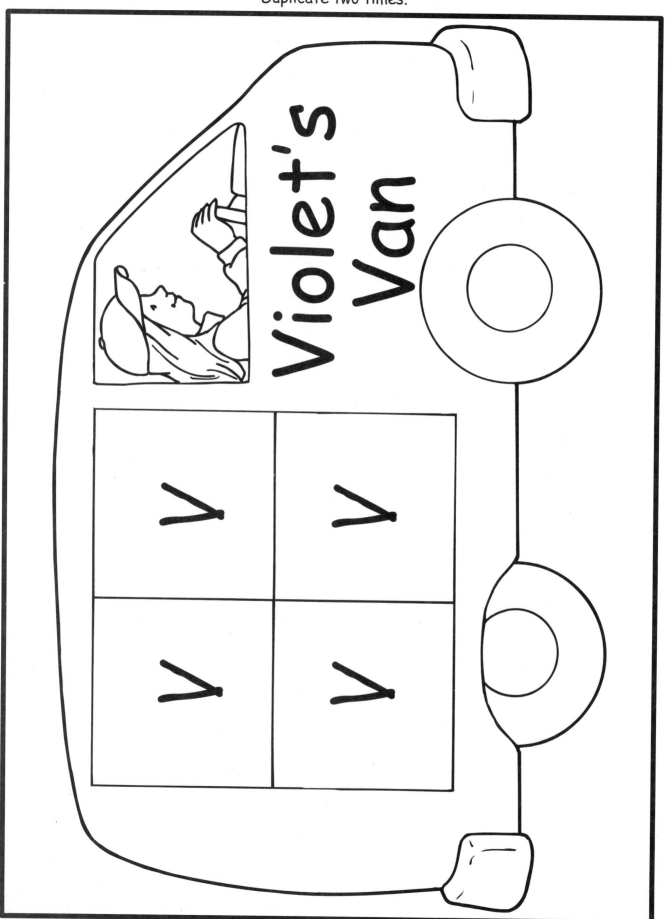

Violet's Van

Vote
☐ Pat
☑ Dan
☐ Ed

Be Mine

WINGO

(Initial Consonant w)

To Play:

Two players may play. Take out the WINGO playing card and the picture cards. Place the cards on the WINGO spaces face up in any order. Each player takes a set of colored markers. Each player in turn puts down a marker on a picture card and names the picture with the initial w sound. The first player to place his/her markers three in a row down, across, or diagonally is the winner. To play again, mix the picture cards on the playing card.

To Make:

Duplicate the WINGO playing card and the picture cards. Glue to oak tag. Cut out the picture cards. Provide 18 colored markers, 9 each of two colors. Enclose the playing card, the picture cards, and the markers in a clasp envelope. Cut out the playing directions and glue to the front of the envelope.

KinderSounds: Games © 2001 Monday Morning Books, Inc.

WINGO

Provide markers.

WINGO

W	W	W
W	W	W
W	W	W

WINGO

Yolanda's Yo-yos

Yolanda's Yo-yos

Initial Consonant y

To Play:

The player names the pictures on the right side of the playing card. If a picture name begins with the y sound, the player inserts one of the shoelaces or pieces of yarn from a Y yo-yo into the hole next to the picture. There are four matching lace-ups. One picture name does not begin with the y sound. Each player should unlace the card before storing it away in its envelope.

To Make:

Duplicate the lace-up for Yolanda's Yo-yos. Glue to oak tag. Color and trim. Punch holes where indicated. Insert shoelaces or colored yarn into the holes next to the yo-yos and knot in the back. Cover loose ends with a bit of tape to prevent fraying. Enclose the playing card in a clasp envelope. Duplicate the game directions and cut out. Glue to the front of the envelope.

Yolanda's Yo-yos

Zip to the Zoo

(Initial Consonant z)

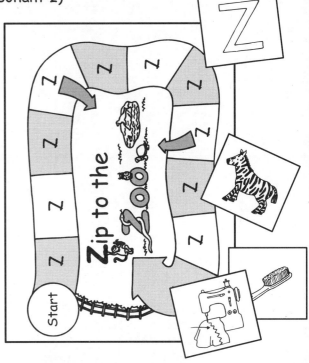

To Play:

Two players may play. Set up the game in the playing area. Take out the die, markers, and picture cards. Mix the picture cards. Place them in rows face down in the playing area. Each player chooses a Zip to the Zoo card to play. Each player takes a marker and places it on Start. Each player in turn throws the die and takes a picture card. The player names the picture on the card. If the picture name begins with the z sound, the player advances his/her marker the number of spaces indicated on the die. If the picture name does not begin with the z sound, the player may not advance the marker. If a player lands on a space with an arrow, he/she follows the arrow and zips to the zoo. The first player to zip to the zoo is the winner.

To Make:

Make two copies of the Zip to the Zoo game set-up. Color and trim. Glue to oak tag. Duplicate the picture cards and glue to oak tag. Cut out the cards and place them with the game set-ups in a clasp envelope. Enclose a die and two markers in the envelope. Duplicate the game directions and cut out. Glue to the front of the envelope.

Zip to the Zoo

Provide a die and two markers.
Duplicate two times.

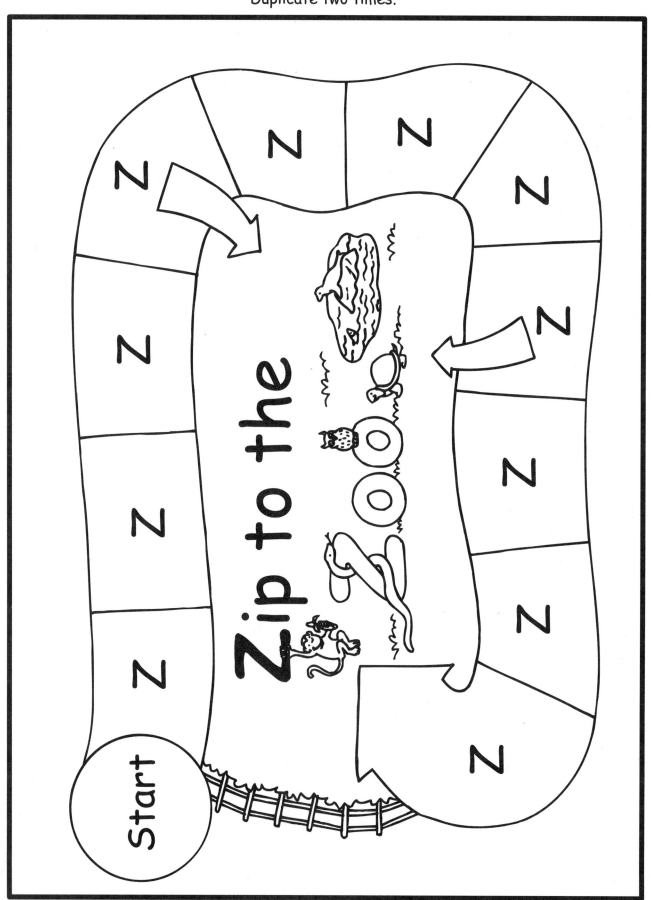

Zip to the Zoo

Apple Slider
(Initial short vowel a)

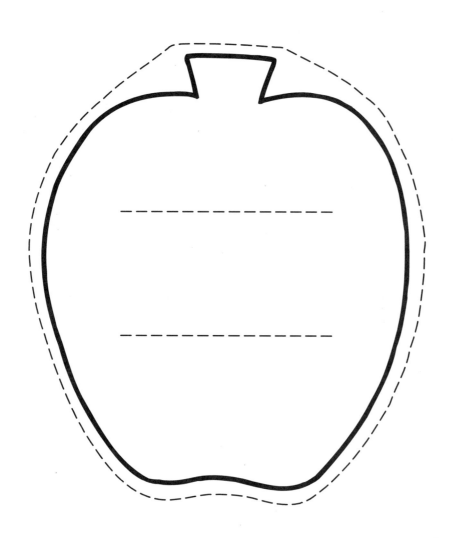

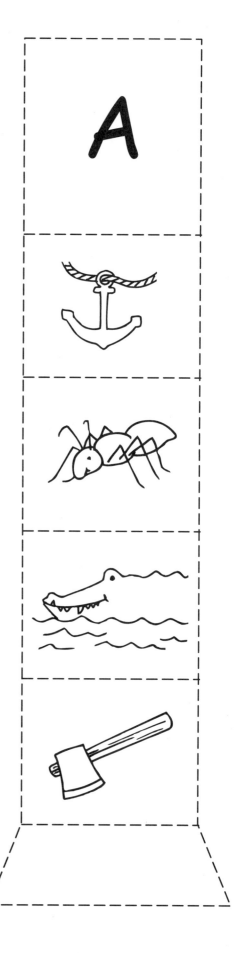

To Play: Slide the slider up on the apple. Name each picture that shows in the window that begins with the short vowel a as in apple. Slide the slider back down and name them again.

To Make: See Specific Directions on page 8.

Elephant Slider

(Initial short vowel e)

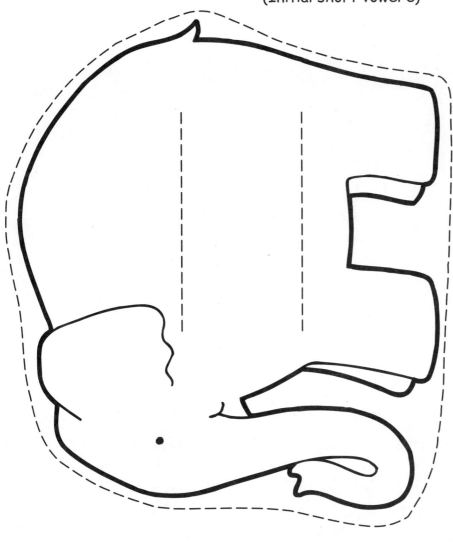

E

To Play: Slide the slider up on the elephant. Name each picture that shows in the window that begins with the short vowel e as in elephant. Slide the slider back down and name them again.

To Make: See Specific Directions on page 8.

Igloo Slider

(Initial short vowel i)

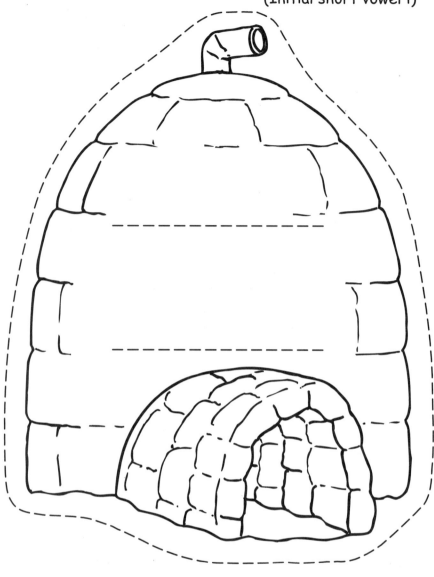

To Play: Slide the slider up on the igloo. Name each picture that shows in the window that begins with the short vowel i as in igloo. Slide the slider back down and name them again.

To Make: See Specific Directions on page 8.

Octopus Slider

(Initial short vowel o)

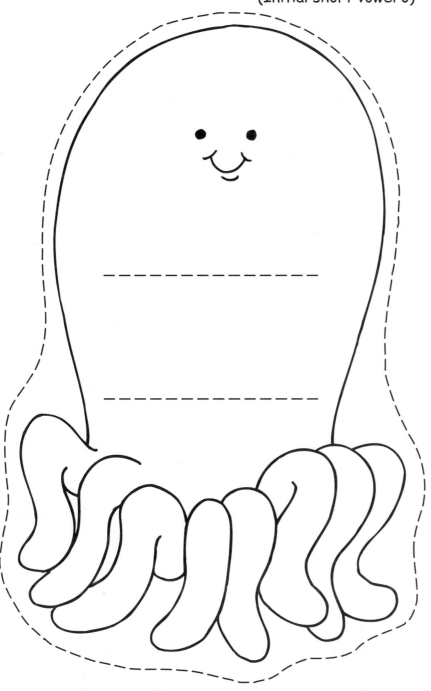

To Play: Slide the slider up on the octopus. Name each picture that shows in the window that begins with the short vowel o as in octopus. Slide the slider back down and name them again.

To Make: See Specific Directions on page 8.

Umbrella Slider

(Initial short vowel u)

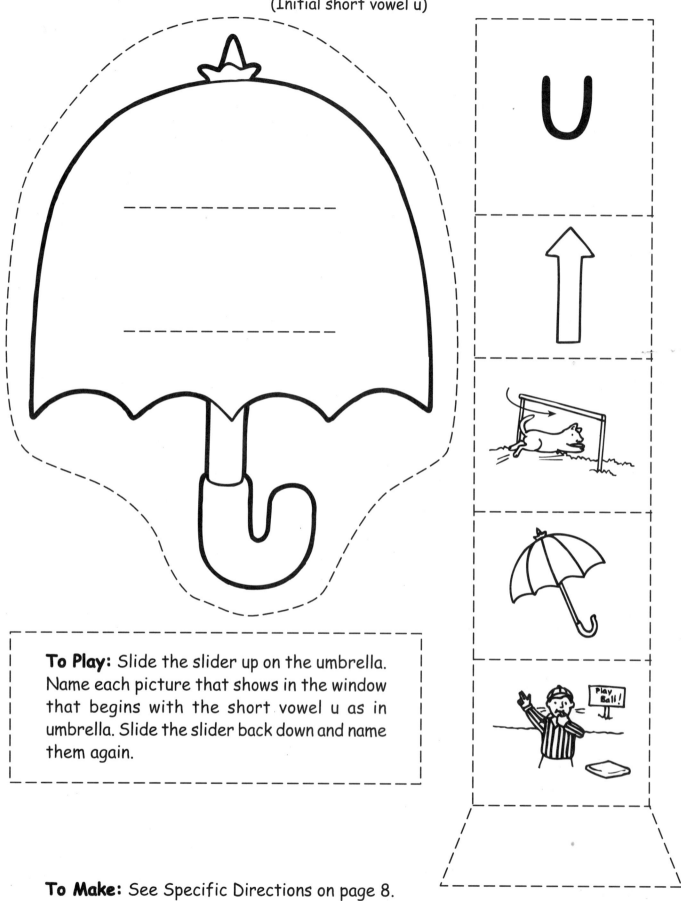

To Play: Slide the slider up on the umbrella. Name each picture that shows in the window that begins with the short vowel u as in umbrella. Slide the slider back down and name them again.

To Make: See Specific Directions on page 8.